DATE DUE

MAY 1992			

A Patriotic Anthology

A Patriotic Anthology

Being poems of American
History, written by great
American poets &

Granger Index Reprint Series

BOOKS FOR LIBRARIES PRESS
FREEPORT, NEW YORK

First Published 1940
Reprinted 1971

INTERNATIONAL STANDARD BOOK NUMBER
0-8369-6306-7

LIBRARY OF CONGRESS CATALOG CARD NUMBER
79-168786

PRINTED IN THE UNITED STATES OF AMERICA
BY
NEW WORLD BOOK MANUFACTURING CO., INC.
HALLANDALE, FLORIDA 33009

THE CONTENTS

A PATRIOTIC ANTHOLOGY

Paul Revere's Ride

LISTEN, my children, and you shall hear
Of the midnight ride of Paul Revere,
On the eighteenth of April, in Seventy-Five:
Hardly a man is now alive
Who remembers that famous day and year.

He said to his friend, "If the British march
By land or sea from the town to-night,
Hang a lantern aloft in the belfry arch
Of the North Church tower as a signal-light,
One, if by land, and two, if by sea;
And I on the opposite shore will be,
Ready to ride and spread the alarm
Through every Middlesex village and farm,
For the country folk to be up and to arm.

Then he said, Good night! and with muffled oar
Silently rowed to the Charlestown shore,
Just as the moon rose over the bay,
Where swinging wide at her moorings lay
The Somerset, British man-of-war;
A phantom ship, with each mast and spar

Across the moon like a prison bar,
And a huge black hulk, that was magnified
By its own reflection in the tide.

Meanwhile, his friend, through alley and street
Wanders and watches with eager ears,
Till in the silence around him he hears
The muster of men at the barrack door,
The sound of arms, and the tramp of feet,
And the measured tread of the grenadiers,
Marching down to their boats on the shore.

Then he climbed to the tower of the Old North
        Church,
By the wooden stairs, with stealthy tread,
To the belfry-chamber overhead,
And startled the pigeons from their perch
On the sombre rafters, that round him made
Masses and moving shapes of shade,—
By the trembling ladder, steep and tall,
To the highest window in the wall,
Where he paused to listen and look down
A moment on the roofs of the town,
And the moonlight flowing over all.

Beneath, in the churchyard, lay the dead,
In their night-encampment on the hill,
Wrapped in silence so deep and still
That he could hear, like a sentinel's tread,
The watchful night-wind, as it went
Creeping along from tent to tent,

And seeming to whisper, "All is well!"
A moment only he feels the spell
Of the place and the hour, and the secret dread
Of the lonely belfry and the dead;
For suddenly all his thoughts are bent
On a shadowy something far away,
Where the river widens to meet the bay,—
A line of black that bends and floats
On the rising tide, like a bridge of boats.

Meanwhile, impatient to mount and ride,
Booted and spurred, with a heavy stride
On the opposite shore walked Paul Revere.
Now he patted his horse's side,
Now gazed at the landscape far and near,
Then, impetuous, stamped the earth,
And turned and tightened his saddle-girth:
But mostly he watched with eager search
The belfry-tower of the Old North Church,
As it rose above the graves on the hill,
Lonely, and spectral, and sombre and still.
And lo! as he looks, on the belfry's height
A glimmer, and then a beam of light!
He springs to the saddle, the bridle he turns
But lingers and gazes, till full on his sight
A second lamp in the belfry burns!
A hurry of hoofs in a village street,
A shape in the moonlight, a bulk in the dark,
And beneath, from the pebbles, in passing, a spark

Struck out by a steed flying fearless and fleet:
That was all! And yet, through the gloom and the
      light,
The fate of a nation was riding that night;
And the spark struck out by that steed, in his flight,
Kindled the land into flame with its heat.

He has left the village and mounted the steep,
And beneath him, tranquil and broad and deep,
Is the Mystic, meeting the ocean tides;
And under the alders, that skirt its edge,
Now soft on the sand, now loud on the ledge,
Is heard the tramp of his steed as he rides.

It was twelve by the village clock
When he crossed the bridge into Medford town
He heard the crowing of the cock,
And the barking of the farmer's dog,
And felt the damp of the river fog.

It was one by the village clock,
When he rode into Lexington.
He saw the gilded weathercock
Swim in the moonlight as he passed,
And the meeting-house windows, blank and bare,
Gaze at him with a spectral glare,
As if they already stood aghast
At the bloody work they would look upon.

It was two by the village clock,
When he came to the bridge in Concord town.
He heard the bleating of the flock,

And the twitter of birds among the trees,
And felt the breath of the morning breeze
Blowing over the meadows brown.
And one was safe and asleep in his bed
Who at the bridge would be first to fall,
Who that day would be lying dead,
Pierced by a British musket-ball.
You know the rest. In the books you have read,
How the British Regulars fired and fled,—
How the farmers gave them ball for ball,
From behind each fence and farm-yard wall,
Chasing the red-coats down the lane,
Then crossing the fields to emerge again
Under the trees at the turn of the road,
And only pausing to fire and load.

So through the night rode Paul Revere;
And so through the night went his cry of alarm
To every Middlesex village and farm,—
A cry of defiance and not of fear,
A voice in the darkness, a knock at the door,
And a word that shall echo forevermore!
For, borne on the night-wind of the Past,
Through all our history, to the last,
In the hour of darkness and peril and need,
The people will waken and listen to hear
The hurrying hoof-beats of that steed,
And the midnight message of Paul Revere.

HENRY WADSWORTH LONGFELLOW

☆ 11 ☆

Hymn

By the rude bridge that arched the flood,
　Their flag to April's breeze unfurled,
Here once the embattled farmers stood,
　And fired the shot heard round the world.

The foe long since in silence slept;
　Alike the conqueror silent sleeps;
And Time the ruined bridge has swept
　Down the dark stream which seaward creeps.

On this green bank, by this soft stream,
　We set to-day a votive stone;
That memory may their deed redeem,
　When, like our sires, our sons are gone.

Spirit, that made those heroes dare
　To die, or leave their children free,
Bid Time and Nature gently spare
　The shaft we raise to them and thee.

RALPH WALDO EMERSON

Grandmother's Story

OF BUNKER HILL BATTLE

'T IS like stirring living embers when, at eighty,
    one remembers
All the achings and the quakings of "the times that
    tried men's souls";
When I talk of *Whig* and *Tory*, when I tell the
    Rebel story,
To you the words are ashes, but to me they 're
    burning coals.

I had heard the muskets' rattle of the April running
    battle;
Lord Percy's hunted soldiers, I can see their red
    coats still;
But a deadly chill comes o'er me, as the day looms
    up before me,
When a thousand men lay bleeding on the slopes of
    Bunker's Hill.

'T was a peaceful summer's morning, when the
    first thing gave us warning
Was the booming of the cannon from the river and
    the shore:

"Child," says grandma, "what 's the matter, what is all this noise and clatter?
Have those scalping Indian devils come to murder us once more?"

Poor old soul! my sides were shaking in the midst of all my quaking
To hear her talk of Indians when the guns began to roar:
She had seen the burning village, and the slaughter and the pillage,
When the Mohawks killed her father, with their bullets through his door.

Then I said, "Now, dear old granny, don't you fret and worry any,
For I 'll soon come back and tell you whether this is work or play;
There can't be mischief in it, so I won't be gone a minute"—
For a minute then I started. I was gone the livelong day.

No time for bodice-lacing or for looking-glass grimacing;
Down my hair went as I hurried, tumbling half-way to my heels;
God forbid your ever knowing, when there 's blood around her flowing,

How the lonely, helpless daughter of a quiet
    household feels!

In the street I heard a thumping; and I knew it was
    the stumping
Of the Corporal, our old neighbor, on that wooden
    leg he wore,
With a knot of women round him,—it was lucky I
    had found him,—
So I followed with the others, and the Corporal
    marched before.

They were making for the steeple,—the old soldier
    and his people;
The pigeons circled round us as we climbed the
    creaking stair,
Just across the narrow river—O, so close it made
    me shiver!—
Stood a fortress on the hill-top that but yesterday
    was bare.

Not slow our eyes to find it; well we knew who
    stood behind it,
Though the earthwork hid them from us, and the
    stubborn walls were dumb:
Here were sister, wife, and mother, looking wild
    upon each other,
And their lips were white with terror as they said
    THE HOUR HAS COME!

The morning slowly wasted, not a morsel had we
tasted,
And our heads were almost splitting with the
cannons' deafening thrill,
When a figure tall and stately round the rampart
strode sedately;
It was PRESCOTT, one since told me; he commanded
on the hill.

Every woman's heart grew bigger when we saw
his manly figure,
With the banyan buckled round it, standing up so
straight and tall;
Like a gentleman of leisure who is strolling out for
pleasure,
Through the storm of shells and cannon-shot he
walked around the wall.

At eleven the streets were swarming, for the red-
coats' ranks were forming;
At noon in marching order they were moving to
the piers;
How the bayonets gleamed and glistened, as we
looked far down and listened
To the trampling and the drum-beat of the belted
grenadiers!

At length the men have started, with a cheer (it
seemed faint-hearted),

In their scarlet regimentals, with their knapsacks
        on their backs,
And the reddening, rippling water, as after a sea-
        fight's slaughter,
Round the barges gliding onward blushed like
        blood along their tracks.

So they crossed to the other border, and again they
        formed in order;
And the boats came back for soldiers, came for
        soldiers, soldiers still:
The time seemed everlasting to us women faint
        and fasting,—
At last they 're moving, marching, marching
        proudly up the hill.

We can see the bright steel glancing all along the
        lines advancing—
Now the front rank fires a volley—they have
        thrown away their shot;
For behind the earthwork lying, all the balls above
        them flying,
Our people need not hurry; so they wait and an-
        swer not.

Then the Corporal, our old cripple (he would
        swear sometimes and tipple),—
He had heard the bullets whistle (in the old French
        war) before,—

Calls out in words of jeering, just as if they all were
    hearing,—
And his wooden leg thumps fiercely on the dusty
    belfry floor:—

"Oh! fire away, ye villains, and earn King George's
    shillin's,
But ye'll waste a ton of powder afore a 'rebel'
    falls.
You may bang the dirt and welcome, they 're as
    safe as Dan'l Malcolm
Ten foot beneath the gravestone that you 've
    splintered with your balls!"

In the hush of expectation, in the awe and trepi-
    dation
Of the dread approaching moment, we are well-
    nigh breathless all;
Though the rotten bars are failing on the rickety
    belfry railing,
We are crowding up against them like the waves
    against a wall.

Just a glimpse (the air is clearer), they are nearer,
    —nearer,—nearer,
When a flash—a curling smoke-wreath—then a
    crash—the steeple shakes—

The deadly truce is ended; the tempest's shroud is
      rended;
Like a morning mist it gathered, like a thunder-
      cloud it breaks!

O the sight our eyes discover as the blue-black
      smoke blows over!
The red-coats stretched in windrows as a mower
      rakes his hay;
Here a scarlet heap is lying, there a headlong
      crowd is flying
Like a billow that has broken and is shivered into
      spray.

Then we cried, "The troops are routed! they are
      beat—it can't be doubted!
God be thanked, the fight is over!"—Ah! the grim
      old soldier's smile!
"Tell us, tell us why you look so?" (we could
      hardly speak, we shook so),—
"Are they beaten? *Are* they beaten? ARE they
      beaten?"—"Wait a while."

O the trembling and the terror! for too soon we
      saw our error:
They are baffled, not defeated; we have driven
      them back in vain:
And the columns that were scattered, round the
      colors that were tattered,

Toward the sullen silent fortress turn their belted
    breasts again.

All at once, as we are gazing, lo the roofs of
    Charlestown blazing!
They have fired the harmless village; in an hour it
    will be down!
The Lord in heaven confound them, rain his fire
    and brimstone round them,—
The robbing, murdering red-coats, that would
    burn a peaceful town!

They are marching, stern and solemn; we can see
    each massive column
As they near the naked earth-mound with the
    slanting walls so steep.
Have our soldiers got faint-hearted, and in noise-
    less haste departed?
Are they panic-struck and helpless? Are they pal-
    sied or asleep?

Now! the walls they 're almost under! scarce a rod
    the foes asunder!
Not a firelock flashed against them! up the earth-
    work they will swarm!
But the words have scarce been spoken, when the
    ominous calm is broken,
And a bellowing crash has emptied all the ven-
    geance of the storm!

So again, with murderous slaughter, pelted back-
   ward to the water,
Fly Pigot's running heroes and the frightened
   braves of Howe;
And we shout, "At last they 're done for, it 's their
   barges they have run for:
They are beaten, beaten, beaten; and the battle's
   over now!"

And we looked, poor timid creatures, on the rough
   old soldier's features,
Our lips afraid to question, but he knew what we
   would ask:
"Not sure," he said; "keep quiet,—once more, I
   guess, they 'll try it—
Here 's damnation to the cut-throats!"—then he
   handed me his flask,

Saying, "Gal, you 're looking shaky; have a drop
   of old Jamaiky;
I 'm afraid there 'll be more trouble afore this job
   is done";
So I took one scorching swallow; dreadful faint I
   felt and hollow,
Standing there from early morning when the fir-
   ing was begun.

All through those hours of trial I had watched a
   calm clock dial,

As the hands kept creeping, creeping,—they were
      creeping round to four,
When the old man said, "They 're forming with
      their bayonets fixed for storming:
It 's the death grip that's a coming,—they will try
      the works once more."

With brazen trumpets blaring, the flames behind
      them glaring,
The deadly wall before them, in close array they
      come;
Still onward, upward toiling, like a dragon's fold
      uncoiling—
Like the rattlesnake's shrill warning the reverberat-
      ing drum!

Over heaps all torn and gory—shall I tell the fearful
      story,
How they surged above the breastwork, as a sea
      breaks over a deck;
How, driven, yet scarce defeated, our worn-out
      men retreated,
With their powder-horns all emptied, like the
      swimmers from a wreck?

It has all been told and painted; as for me, they say
      I fainted,
And the wooden-legged old Corporal stumped
      with me down the stair:

When I woke from dreams affrighted the evening
      lamps were lighted,—
On the floor a youth was lying; his bleeding breast
      was bare.

And I heard through all the flurry, "Send for
      WARREN! hurry! hurry!
Tell him here 's a soldier bleeding, and he 'll come
      and dress his wound!"
Ah, we knew not till the morrow told its tale of
      death and sorrow,
How the starlight found him stiffened on the dark
      and bloody ground.

Who the youth was, what his name was, where the
      place from which he came was,
Who had brought him from the battle, and had
      left him at our door,
He could not speak to tell us; but 't was one of our
      brave fellows,
As the homespun plainly showed us which the
      dying soldier wore.

For they all thought he was dying, as they gath-
      ered 'round him crying,—
And they said, "O, how they 'll miss him!" and,
      "What will his mother do?"
Then, his eyelids just unclosing like a child's that
      has been dozing,

He faintly murmured, "Mother!"——and—I saw
      his eyes were blue.

—"Why, grandma, how you 're winking!"—Ah,
      my child, it sets me thinking
Of a story not like this one. Well, he somehow
      lived along;
So we came to know each other, and I nursed him
      like a—mother,
Till at last he stood before me, tall and rosy-
      cheeked, and strong.

And we sometimes walked together in the pleasant
      summer weather;
—"Please to tell us what his name was?"—Just your
      own, my little dear,—
There 's his picture Copley painted: we became so
      well acquainted,
That—in short, that 's why I'm grandma, and you
      children all are here!

OLIVER WENDELL HOLMES

Warren's Address

STAND! the ground 's your own, my braves!
   Will ye give it up to slaves?
Will ye look for greener graves?
      Hope ye mercy still?
What 's the mercy despots feel?
Hear it in that battle-peal!
Read it on yon bristling steel,
      Ask it,—ye who will.

Fear ye foes who kill for hire?
Will ye to your *homes* retire?
Look behind you! they 're a-fire!
      And, before you, see
Who have done it!—From the vale
On they come!—And will ye quail?—
Leaden rain and iron hail
Let their welcome be!

In the God of battles trust!
Die we may,—and die we must;—
But, O, where can dust to dust

Be consigned so well,
As where Heaven its dews shall shed
On the martyred patriot's bed,
And the rocks shall raise their head,
Of his deeds to tell!

JOHN PIERPONT

Song of Marion's Men

OUR band is few, but true and tried,
  Our leader frank and bold;
The British soldier trembles
  When Marion's name is told.
Our fortress is the good greenwood
  Our tent the cypress-tree;
We know the forest round us,
  As seamen know the sea.
We know its walls of thorny vines,
  Its glades of reedy grass,
Its safe and silent islands
  Within the dark morass.

Wo to the English soldiery,
  That little dread us near!
On them shall light at midnight
  A strange and sudden fear:
When, waking to their tents on fire
  They grasp their arms in vain,
And they who stand to face us
  Are beat to earth again.

And they who fly in terror deem
    A mighty host behind,
And hear the tramp of thousands
    Upon the hollow wind.

Then sweet the hour that brings release
    From danger and from toil;
We talk the battle over,
    And share the battle's spoil.
The woodland rings with laugh and shout,
    As if a hunt were up,
And woodland flowers are gathered
    To crown the soldier's cup.
With merry songs we mock the wind
    That in the pine-top grieves,
And slumber long and sweetly
    On beds of oaken leaves.

Well knows the fair and friendly moon
    The band that Marion leads—
The glitter of their rifles,
    The scampering of their steeds.
'Tis life to guide the fiery barb
    Across the moonlight plain;
'Tis life to feel the night-wind
    That lifts his tossing mane.
A moment in the British camp—
    A moment—and away
Back to the pathless forest,
    Before the peep of day.

☆ 28 ☆

Grave men there are by broad Santee,
   Grave men with hoary hairs;
Their hearts are all with Marion,
   For Marion are their prayers.
And lovely ladies greet our band
   With kindliest welcoming,
With smiles like those of summer,
   And tears like those of spring.
For them we wear these trusty arms,
   And lay them down no more
Till we have driven the Briton,
   For ever, from our shore.

WILLIAM CULLEN BRYANT

The Star-Spangled Banner

O<small>H</small>! say can you see, by the dawn's early light,
What so proudly we hailed at the twilight's last
gleaming;
Whose broad stripes and bright stars through the
perilous fight,
O'er the ramparts we watched, were so gallantly
streaming?
And the rocket's red glare, the bombs bursting in air,
Gave proof through the night that our flag was still
there,
Oh, say, does that star-spangled banner yet wave
O'er the land of the free and the home of the brave?

On the shore, dimly seen through the mists of the
deep,
Where the foe's haughty host in dread silence
reposes,
What is that which the breeze o'er the towering
steep
As it fitfully blows, half conceals, half discloses?

Now it catches the gleam of the morning's first
      beam;
Its full glory reflected now shines on the stream;
'T is the star-spangled banner! Oh! long may it wave
O'er the land of the free and the home of the brave!

And where is the band who so vauntingly swore,
Mid the havoc of war and the battle's confusion,
A home and a country they 'd leave us no more?
Their blood hath washed out their foul footsteps'
      pollution;
No refuge could save the hireling and slave
From the terror of flight, or the gloom of the grave,
And the star-spangled banner in triumph doth wave
O'er the land of the free and the home of the brave!

Oh! thus be it ever, when freemen shall stand
Between their loved home and the war's desolation;
Blessed with victory and peace, may the Heaven-
      rescued land
Praise the Power that hath made and preserved us a
      nation.
Then conquer we must, for our cause it is just,
And this be our motto, "In God is our trust":
And the star-spangled banner in triumph shall wave
O'er the land of the free and the home of the brave.

FRANCIS SCOTT KEY

The American Flag

WHEN Freedom, from her mountain height,
Unfurled her standard to the air,
She tore the azure robe of night,
    And set the stars of glory there!
She mingled with its gorgeous dyes
The milky baldric of the skies,
And striped its pure celestial white
With streakings of the morning light,
Then, from his mansion in the sun,
She called her eagle-bearer down,
And gave into his mighty hand
The symbol of her chosen land!

Majestic monarch of the cloud!
    Who rear'st aloft thy regal form,
To hear the tempest-tramping loud,
And see the lightning-lances driven,
    When stride the warriors of the storm,
And rolls the thunder-drum of heaven!
Child of the sun! to thee 'tis given
    To guard the banner of the free,

To hover in the sulphur smoke,
To ward away the battle stroke,
And bid its blendings shine afar,
Like rainbows on the cloud of war,
   The harbingers of victory!

Flag of the brave! thy folds shall fly,
The sign of hope and triumph high!
When speaks the signal-trumpet tone,
And the long line comes gleaming on,
(Ere yet the life-blood, warm and wet,
Has dimmed the glist'ning bayonet),
Each soldier's eye shall brightly turn
To where thy meteor-glories burn,
And, as his springing steps advance,
Catch war and vengeance from the glance!
And when the cannon-mouthings loud
Heave in wild wreaths the battle-shroud,
And gory sabres rise and fall,
Like shoots of flame on midnight's pall!
There shall thy victor-glances glow,
   And cowering foes shall shrink beneath,
Each gallant arm that strikes below,
   The lovely messenger of death.

Flag of the seas! on ocean's wave
Thy star shall glitter o'er the brave;
When Death, careering on the gale,
Sweeps darkly round the bellied sail,

And frighted waves rush wildly back
Before the broad-side's reeling rack,
The dying wanderer of the sea
Shall look, at once, to heaven and thee,
And smile, to see thy splendors fly,
In triumph, o'er his closing eye.

Flag of the free heart's hope and home,
   By angel hands to valor given!
Thy stars have lit the welkin dome,
   And all thy hues were born in heaven!
[And fixed as yonder orb divine,
   That saw thy bannered blaze unfurled,
Shall thy proud stars resplendent shine,
   The guard and glory of the world.]
Forever float that standard sheet!
   Where breathes the foe but falls before us?
With Freedom's soil beneath our feet,
   And Freedom's banner streaming o'er us!

JOSEPH RODMAN DRAKE

Old Ironsides

Ay, tear her tattered ensign down!
  Long has it waved on high,
And many an eye has danced to see
  That banner in the sky;
Beneath it rung the battle shout,
  And burst the cannon's roar;—
The meteor of the ocean air
  Shall sweep the clouds no more!

Her deck, once red with heroes' blood,
  Where knelt the vanquished foe,
When winds were hurrying o'er the flood
  And waves were white below,
No more shall feel the victor's tread,
  Or know the conquered knee;—
The harpies of the shore shall pluck
  The eagle of the sea!

Oh, better that her shattered hulk
  Should sink beneath the wave;
Her thunders shook the mighty deep,

And there should be her grave;
Nail to the mast her holy flag,
    Set every threadbare sail,
And give her to the God of storms,—
    The lightning and the gale!

OLIVER WENDELL HOLMES

The Bivouac of the Dead

THE muffled drum's sad roll has beat
  The soldier's last tattoo;
No more on life's parade shall meet
  That brave and fallen few.
On fame's eternal camping ground
  Their silent tents are spread,
And glory guards, with solemn round,
  The bivouac of the dead.

No rumor of the foe's advance
  Now swells upon the wind;
No troubled thought at midnight haunts
  Of loved ones left behind;
No vision of the morrow's strife
  The warrior's dream alarms;
No braying horn, nor screaming fife,
  At dawn shall call to arms.

Their shivered swords are red with rust,
  Their pluméd heads are bowed;
Their haughty banner, trailed in dust,

Is now their martial shroud.
And plenteous funeral tears have washed
  The red stains from each brow,
And the proud forms, by battle gashed,
  Are free from anguish now.

The neighing troop, the flashing blade,
  The bugle's stirring blast,
The charge, the dreadful cannonade,
  The din and shout are past;
Nor war's wild note nor glory's peal
  Shall thrill with fierce delight
Those breasts that never more may feel
  The rapture of the fight.

*   *   *

Sons of the Dark and Bloody Ground,
  Ye must not slumber there,
Where stranger steps and tongues resound
  Along the heedless air;
Your own proud land's heroic soil
  Shall be your fitter grave;
She claims from war his richest spoil—
  The ashes of her brave.

So, 'neath their parent turf they rest,
  Far from the gory field,
Borne to a Spartan mother's breast,

On many a bloody shield;
The sunshine of their native sky
  Smiles sadly on them here,
And kindred eyes and hearts watch by
  The heroes' sepulchre.

Rest on, embalmed and sainted dead,
  Dear as the blood ye gave;
No impious footstep here shall tread
  The herbage of your grave;
Nor shall your glory be forgot
  While Fame her record keeps,
Or Honor points the hallowed spot
  Where Valor proudly sleeps.

Yon marble minstrel's voiceless stone,
  In deathless song shall tell,
When many a vanished age hath flown
  The story how ye fell;
Nor wreck, nor change, nor winter's blight,
  Nor Time's remorseless doom,
Shall dim one ray of glory's light
  That gilds your deathless tomb.

THEODORE O'HARA

Scott and the Veteran

An old and crippled veteran to the War Department
came;
He sought the Chief who led him on many a field of
fame,—
The Chief who shouted "Forward!" where'er his
banner rose,
And bore its stars in triumph behind the flying foes.

"Have you forgotten, General," the battered soldier
cried,
"The days of Eighteen Hundred Twelve, when I
was at your side?
Have you forgotten Johnson, that fought at Lundy's
Lane?
'T is true, I'm old and pensioned, but I want to fight
again."

"Have I forgotten?" said the Chief; "my brave old
soldier, No!
And here's the hand I gave you then, and let it tell
you so:

But you have done your share, my friend; you're
        crippled, old, and gray,
And we have need of younger arms and fresher
        blood to-day."

"But, General," cried the veteran, a flush upon his
        brow,
"The very men who fought with us, they say, are
        traitors now;
They've torn the flag of Lundy's Lane,—our old
        red, white, and blue;
And while a drop of blood is left, I'll show that
        drop is true.

"I'm not so weak but I can strike, and I've a good
        old gun
To get the range of traitors' hearts, and pick them,
        one by one.
Your Minié rifles, and such arms, it a'n't worth
        while to try:
I couldn't get the hang o' them, but I'll keep my
        powder dry!"

"God bless you, comrade!" said the Chief; "God
        bless your loyal heart!
But younger men are in the field, and claim to have
        their part;
They 'll plant our sacred banner in each rebellious
        town,

And woe, henceforth, to any hand that dares to pull
      it down!''   .

"But, General,"—still persisting, the weeping veteran
      cried,
"I'm young enough to follow, so long as you're my
      guide;
And some, you know, must bite the dust, and that, at
      least, can I,—
So give the young ones place to fight, but me a place
      to die!

"If they should fire on Pickens, let the Colonel in
      command
Put me upon the rampart, with the flag-staff in my
      hand:
No odds how hot the cannon-smoke, or how the
      shell may fly;
I'll hold the Stars and Stripes aloft, and hold them
      till I die!

"I'm ready, General, so you let a post to me be given,
Where Washington can see me, as he looks from
      highest heaven,
And say to Putnam at his side, or, may be, General
      Wayne:
'There stands old Billy Johnson, that fought at
      Lundy's Lane!'

"And when the fight is hottest, before the traitors fly,
When shell and ball are screeching and bursting in the
      sky,
If any shot should hit me, and lay me on my face,
My soul would go to Washington's, and not to
      Arnold's place!"

BAYARD TAYLOR

The Picket Guard

"ALL quiet along the Potomac," they say,
   "Except now and then a stray picket
Is shot, as he walks on his beat, to and fro,
   By a rifleman hid in the thicket.
'T is nothing—a private or two, now and then,
   Will not count in the news of the battle;
Not an officer lost—only one of the men,
   Moaning out, all alone, the death rattle."

All quiet along the Potomac to-night,
   Where the soldiers lie peacefully dreaming;
Their tents in the rays of the clear autumn moon,
   Or the light of the watch-fires, are gleaming.
A tremulous sigh, as the gentle night-wind
   Through the forest-leaves softly is creeping;
While stars up above, with their glittering eyes,
   Keep guard—for the army is sleeping.

There's only the sound of the lone sentry's tread
   As he tramps from the rock to the fountain,
And thinks of the two in the low trundle-bed

Far away in the cot on the mountain.
His musket falls slack—his face, dark and grim,
  Grows gentle with memories tender,
As he mutters a prayer for the children asleep—
  For their mother—may Heaven defend her!

The moon seems to shine just as brightly as then,
  That night, when the love yet unspoken
Leaped up to his lips—when low-murmured vows
  Were pledged to be ever unbroken.
Then drawing his sleeve roughly over his eyes,
  He dashes off tears that are welling,
And gathers his gun closer up to its place
  As if to keep down the heart-swelling.

He passes the fountain, the blasted pine-tree—
  The footstep is lagging and weary;
Yet onward he goes, through the broad belt of light,
  Toward the shades of the forest so dreary.
Hark! was it the night-wind that rustled the leaves?
  Was it moonlight so wondrously flashing?
It looked like a rifle—"Ah! Mary, good-bye!"
  And the life-blood is ebbing and plashing.

All quiet along the Potomac to-night,
  No sound save the rush of the river;
While soft falls the dew on the face of the dead—
  The picket 's off duty forever.

ETHEL LYNN BEERS

☆ 45 ☆

At Port Royal

THE tent-lights glimmer on the land,
  The ship-lights on the sea;
The night-wind smooths with drifting sand
  Our track on lone Tybee.

At last our grating keels outslide,
  Our good boats forward swing;
And while we ride the land-locked tide,
  Our negroes row and sing.

For dear the bondman holds his gifts
  Of music and of song:
The gold that kindly Nature sifts
  Among his sands of wrong;

The power to make his toiling days
  And poor home-comforts please;
The quaint relief of mirth that plays
  With sorrow's minor keys.

Another glow than sunset's fire
  Has filled the West with light,

Where field and garner, barn and byre,
   Are blazing through the night.

The land is wild with fear and hate,
   The rout runs mad and fast;
From hand to hand, from gate to gate,
   The flaming brand is passed.

The lurid glow falls strong across
   Dark faces broad with smiles;
Not theirs the terror, hate, and loss
   That fire yon blazing piles.

With oar-strokes timing to their song,
   They weave in simple lays
The pathos of remembered wrong,
   The hope of better days,—

The triumph-note that Miriam sung,
   The joy of uncaged birds:
Softening with Afric's mellow tongue
   Their broken Saxon words.

SONG OF THE NEGRO BOATMEN

O, Praise an' tanks! De Lord he come
   To set de people free;
An' massa tink it day ob doom,
   An' we ob jubilee.

De Lord dat heap de Red Sea waves
　　He jus' as 'trong as den;
He say de word: we las' night slaves;
　　To-day, de Lord's freemen.
De yam will grow, de cotton blow,
　　We 'll hab de rice an' corn:
O nebber you fear, if nebber you hear
　　De driver blow his horn!

Ole massa on he trabbels gone;
　　He leaf de land behind:
De Lord's breff blow him furder on,
　　Like corn-shuck in de wind.
We own de hoe, we own de plough,
　　We own de hands dat hold;
We sell de pig, we sell de cow,
　　But nebber chile be sold.
De yam will grow, de cotton blow,
　　We 'll hab de rice an' corn:
O nebber you fear, if nebber you hear
　　De driver blow his horn!

We pray de Lord: he gib us signs
　　Dat some day we be free;
De norf-wind tell it to de pines,
　　De wild-duck to de sea;
We tink it when de church-bell ring,
　　We dream it in de dream;
De rice-bird mean it when he sing,
　　De eagle when he scream.

De yam will grow, de cotton blow,
   We 'll hab de rice an' corn:
O nebber you fear, if nebber you hear
   De driver blow his horn!

We know de promise nebber fail,
   An' nebber lie de word;
So like de 'postles in de jail,
   We waited for de Lord:
An' now he open ebery door
   An' trow away de key;
He tink we lub him so before,
   We lub him better free.
De yam will grow, de cotton blow,
   He' 'll gib de rice an' corn:
O nebber you fear, if nebber you hear
   De driver blow his horn!

So sing our dusky gondoliers;
   And with a secret pain,
And smiles that seem akin to tears,
   We hear the wild refrain.

We dare not share the negro's trust,
   Nor yet his hope deny;
We only know that God is just,
   And every wrong shall die.

Rude seems the song; each swarthy face,
  Flame-lighted, ruder still:
We start to think that hapless race
  Must shape our good or ill;

That laws of changeless justice bind
  Oppressor with oppressed;
And, close as sin and suffering joined,
  We march to Fate abreast.

Sing on, poor hearts! your chant shall be
  Our sign of blight or doom,—
The Vala-song of Liberty,
  Or death-rune of our doom!

JOHN GREENLEAF WHITTIER

John Burns of Gettysburg

Have you heard the story that gossips tell
Of Burns of Gettysburg?—No? Ah, well:
Brief is the glory that hero earns,
Briefer the story of poor John Burns:
He was the fellow who won renown,—
The only man who did n't back down
When the rebels rode through his native town;
But held his own in the fight next day,
When all his townsfolk ran away.
That was in July, Sixty-three,
The very day that General Lee,
Flower of Southern chivalry,
Baffled and beaten, backward reeled
From a stubborn Meade and a barren field.
I might tell how but the day before
John Burns stood at his cottage door,
Looking down the village street,
Where, in the shade of his peaceful vine,
He heard the low of his gathered kine,
And felt their breath with incense sweet.
Or I might say, when the sunset burned

The old farm gable, he thought it turned
The milk that fell like a babbling flood
Into the milk-pail red as blood!
Or how he fancied the hum of bees
Were bullets buzzing among the trees.
But all such fanciful thoughts as these
Were strange to a practical man like Burns,
Who minded only his own concerns,
Troubled no more by fancies fine
Than one of his calm-eyed, long-tailed, kine,—
Quite old-fashioned and matter-of-fact,
Slow to argue, but quick to act.
That was the reason as some folks say,
He fought so well on that terrible day.

And it was terrible. On the right
Raged for hours the heady fight,
Thundered the battery's double bass,—
Difficult music for men to face;
While on the left—where now the graves
Undulate like the living waves
That all that day unceasing swept
Up to the pits the Rebels kept—
Round shot ploughed the upland glades,
Sown with bullets, reaped with blades;
Shattered fences here and there
Tossed their splinters in the air;
The very trees were stripped and bare;
The barns that once held yellow grain

Were heaped with harvests of the slain;
The cattle bellowed on the plain,
The turkeys screamed with might and main,
And brooding barn-fowl left their rest
With strange shells bursting in each nest.

Just where the tide of battle turns,
Erect and lonely stood old John Burns.
How do you think the man was dressed?
He wore an ancient long buff vest,
Yellow as saffron,—but his best,
And, buttoned over his manly breast,
Was a bright blue coat, with a rolling collar,
And large gilt buttons,—size of a dollar,—
With tails that the country-folk called "swaller."
He wore a broad-brimmed, bell-crowned hat,
White as the locks on which it sat.
Never had such a sight been seen
For forty years on the village green,
Since old John Burns was a country beau,
And went to the "quiltings" long ago.

Close at his elbows all that day,
Veterans of the Peninsula,
Sunburnt and bearded, charged away;
And striplings, downy of lip and chin,—
Clerks that the Home Guard mustered in,—
Glanced, as they passed, at the hat he wore,
Then at the rifle his right hand bore;

And hailed him, from out their youthful lore,
With scraps of a slangy *répertoire:*
"How are you, White Hat?" "Put her through!"
"Your head 's level!" and "Bully for you!"
Called him "Daddy,"—begged he 'd disclose
The name of the tailor who made his clothes,
And what was the value he set on those;
While Burns, unmindful of jeer and scoff,
Stood there picking the rebels off,—
With his long brown rifle and bell-crown hat,
And the swallow-tails they were laughing at.

'T was but a moment, for that respect
Which clothes all courage their voices checked;
And something the wildest could understand
Spake in the old man's strong right hand,
And his corded throat, and the lurking frown
Of his eyebrows under his old bell-crown;
Until, as they gazed, there crept an awe
Through the ranks in whispers, and some men saw,
In the antique vestments and long white hair,
The Past of the Nation in battle there;
And some of the soldiers since declare
That the gleam of his old white hat afar,
Like the crested plume of the brave Navarre,
That day was their oriflamme of war.

So raged the battle. You know the rest:
How the rebels, beaten and backward pressed,

Broke at the final charge, and ran.
At which John Burns—a practical man—
Shouldered his rifle, unbent his brows,
And then went back to his bees and cows.

That is the story of old John Burns;
This is the moral the reader learns:
In fighting the battle, the question 's whether
You 'll show a hat that's white, or a feather!

BRET HARTE

Battle-Hymn of the Republic

MINE eyes have seen the glory of the coming of
the Lord:
He is trampling out the vintage where the grapes of
wrath are stored;
He hath loosed the fateful lightning of His terrible
swift sword:
His truth is marching on.

I have seen Him in the watch-fires of a hundred
circling camps;
They have builded Him an altar in the evening dews
and damps;
I can read His righteous sentence by the dim and
flaring lamps.
His day is marching on.

I have read a fiery gospel, writ in burnished rows of
steel:
"As ye deal with My contemners, so with you My
grace shall deal;

Let the Hero, born of woman, crush the serpent with
     His heel,
     Since God is marching on."

He has sounded forth the trumpet that shall never call
     retreat;
He is sifting out the hearts of men before His
     judgment-seat:
Oh! be swift, my soul, to answer Him! be jubilant, my
     feet!
     Our God is marching on.

In the beauty of the lilies Christ was born across the
     sea,
With a glory in His bosom that transfigures you and
     me:
As He died to make men holy, let us die to make men
     free,
     While God is marching on.

JULIA WARD HOWE

Ready

Loaded with gallant soldiers,
  A boat shot in to the land,
And lay at the right of Rodman's Point
  With her keel upon the sand.

Lightly, gayly, they came to shore,
  And never a man afraid;
When sudden the enemy opened fire
  From his deadly ambuscade.

Each man fell flat on the bottom
  Of the boat; and the captain said:
"If we lie here, we all are captured,
  And the first who moves is dead!"

Then out spoke a negro sailor,
  No slavish soul had he;
"Somebody's got to die, boys,
  And it might as well be me!"

Firmly he rose, and fearlessly
   Stepped out into the tide;
He pushed the vessel safely off,
   Then fell across her side:

Fell, pierced by a dozen bullets,
   As the boat swung clear and free;—
But there wasn't a man of them that day
   Who was fitter to die than he!

PHOEBE CAREY

Barbara Frietchie

Up from the meadows rich with corn,
Clear in the cool September morn.
The clustered spires of Frederick stand
Green-walled by the hills of Maryland.
Round about them orchards sweep,
Apple and peach tree fruited deep,
Fair as a garden of the Lord
To the eyes of the famished rebel horde,
On that pleasant morn of the early fall
When Lee marched over the mountain-wall,—
Over the mountains winding down,
Horse and foot, into Frederick town.

Forty flags with their silver stars,
Forty flags with their crimson bars,
Flapped in the morning wind: the sun
Of noon looked down, and saw not one.
Up rose old Barbara Frietchie then,
Bowed with her fourscore years and ten;
Bravest of all in Frederick town,

She took up the flag the men hauled down;
In her attic window the staff she set,
To show that one heart was loyal yet.

Up the street came the rebel tread,
Stonewall Jackson riding ahead.
Under his slouched hat left and right
He glanced; the old flag met his sight.
"Halt!"—the dust-brown ranks stood fast.
"Fire!"—out blazed the rifle-blast.
It shivered the window, pane and sash;
It rent the banner with seam and gash.
Quick, as it fell, from the broken staff
Dame Barbara snatched the silken scarf;
She leaned far out on the window-sill,
And shook it forth with a royal will.
"Shoot, if you must, this old gray head,
But spare your country's flag," she said.

A shade of sadness, a blush of shame,
Over the face of the leader came;
The nobler nature within him stirred
To life at that woman's deed and word:
"Who touches a hair of yon gray head
Dies like a dog! March on!" he said.

All day long through Frederick street
Sounded the tread of marching feet:
All day long that free flag tost

Over the heads of the rebel host.
Ever its torn folds rose and fell
On the loyal winds that loved it well;
And through the hill-gaps sunset light
Shone over it with a warm good-night.

Barbara Frietchie's work is o'er,
And the Rebel rides on his raids no more.
Honor to her! and let a tear
Fall, for her sake, on Stonewall's bier.
Over Barbara Frietchie's grave,
Flag of Freedom and Union, wave!
Peace and order and beauty draw
Round thy symbol of light and law;
And ever the stars above look down
On thy stars below in Frederick town!

JOHN GREENLEAF WHITTIER

Fredericksburg

THE increasing moonlight drifts across my bed,
 And on the churchyard by the road, I know
It falls as white and noiselessly as snow.
'T was such a night two weary summers fled;
The stars, as now, were waning overhead.
Listen! Again the shrill-lipped bugles blow
Where the swift currents of the river flow
Past Fredericksburg: far off the heavens are red
With sudden conflagration: on yon height,
Linstock in hand, the gunners hold their breath:
A signal-rocket pierces the dense night,
Flings its spent stars upon the town beneath:
Hark!—the artillery massing on the right,
Hark!—the black squadrons wheeling down to
        Death!

THOMAS BAILEY ALDRICH

Sheridan's Ride

Up from the South at break of day,
Bringing to Winchester fresh dismay,
The affrighted air with a shudder bore,
Like a herald in haste, to the chieftain's door,
The terrible grumble, and rumble, and roar,
Telling the battle was on once more,
And Sheridan twenty miles away.

And wider still those billows of war
Thundered along the horizon's bar;
And louder yet into Winchester rolled
The roar of that red sea uncontrolled,
Making the blood of the listener cold,
As he thought of the stake in that fiery fray,
And Sheridan twenty miles away.

But there is a road from Winchester town,
A good, broad highway leading down;
And there, through the flush of the morning light,
A steed as black as the steeds of night,
Was seen to pass, as with eagle flight,

As if he knew the terrible need;
He stretched away with his utmost speed;
Hills rose and fell; but his heart was gay,
With Sheridan fifteen miles away.

Still sprung from those swift hoofs, thundering
      South,
The dust, like smoke from the cannon's mouth;
Or the trail of a comet, sweeping faster and faster,
Foreboding to traitors the doom of disaster.
The heart of the steed and the heart of the master
Were beating like prisoners assaulting their walls,
Impatient to be where the battle-field calls;
Every nerve of the charger was strained to full play,
With Sheridan only ten miles away.

Under his spurning feet the road
Like an arrowy Alpine river flowed,
And the landscape sped away behind
Like an ocean flying before the wind,
And the steed, like a bark fed with furnace fire,
Swept on, with his wild eye full of ire.
But lo! he is nearing his heart's desire;
He is snuffing the smoke of the roaring fray,
With Sheridan only five miles away.

The first that the general saw were the groups
Of stragglers, and then the retreating troops,
What was done? what to do? a glance told him both,

Then striking his spurs, with a terrible oath,
He dashed down the line, mid a storm of huzzas,
And the wave of retreat checked its course there,
    because
The sight of the master compelled it to pause.
With foam and with dust, the black charger was
    gray
By the flash of his eye, and the red nostril's play,
He seemed to the whole great army to say,
"I have brought you Sheridan all the way
From Winchester, down to save the day!"

Hurrah! hurrah for Sheridan!
Hurrah! hurrah for horse and man!
And when their statues are placed on high,
Under the dome of the Union sky,
The American soldiers' Temple of Fame,
There with the glorious general's name
Be it said, in letters both bold and bright,
"Here is the steed that saved the day,
By carrying Sheridan into the fight,
From Winchester, twenty miles away!"

THOMAS BUCHANAN READ

Sherman's March to the Sea

Our camp-fires shone bright on the mountain
  That frowned on the river below,
As we stood by our guns in the morning,
  And eagerly watched for the foe;
When a rider came out of the darkness
  That hung over mountain and tree,
And shouted, "Boys, up and be ready!
  For Sherman will march to the sea!"

Then cheer upon cheer for bold Sherman
  Went up from each valley and glen,
And the bugles re-echoed the music
  That came from the lips of the men;
For we knew that the stars in our banner
  More bright in their splendor would be,
And that blessings from Northland would greet us,
  When Sherman marched down to the sea.

Then forward, boys! forward to battle!
  We marched on our wearisome way,
We stormed the wild hills of Resaca—

God bless those who fell on that day!
Then Kenesaw, dark in its glory,
     Frowned down on the flag of the free;
But the East and the West bore our standard
     And Sherman marched down to the sea.

Still onward we pressed, till our banners
     Swept out from Atlanta's grim walls,
And the blood of the patriot dampened
     The soil where the traitor-flag falls;
We paused not to weep for the fallen,
     Who slept by each river and tree,
Yet we twined them a wreath of the laurel,
     As Sherman marched down to the sea.

Oh, proud was our army that morning,
     That stood where the pine darkly towers,
When Sherman said, "Boys, you are weary,
     But to-day fair Savannah is ours!"
Then sang we the song of our chieftain,
     That echoed o'er river and lea,
And the stars in our banner shone brighter
     When Sherman marched down to the sea.

SAMUEL H. M. BYERS

Oh Captain! My Captain!

O Captain! my Captain! our fearful trip is done,
The ship has weather'd every rack, the prize we
sought is won;
The port is near, the bells I hear, the people all
exulting,
While follow eyes the steady keel, the vessel grim
and daring:
But O heart! heart! heart!
O the bleeding drops of red,
Where on the deck my Captain lies,
Fallen cold and dead!

O Captain! my Captain! rise up and hear the bells;
Rise up—for you the flag is flung—for you the bugle
trills;
For you bouquets and ribbon'd wreaths—for you
the shores a-crowding;
For you they call, the swaying mass, their eager
faces turning;
Here Captain! dear father!

This arm beneath your head;
   It is some dream that on the deck
      You've fallen cold and dead.

My Captain does not answer, his lips are pale and
    still;
My father does not feel my arm, he has no pulse nor
    will:
The ship is anchor'd safe and sound, its voyage
    closed and done;
From fearful trip the victor ship, comes in with
    object won:
    Exult, O shores, and ring, O bells!
    But I, with mournful tread,
      Walk the deck my Captain lies,
        Fallen cold and dead.

WALT WHITMAN

Abraham Lincoln

Such was he, our Martyr-Chief,
  Whom late the Nation he had led,
    With ashes on her head,
Wept with the passion of an angry grief:
Forgive me, if from present things I turn
To speak what in my heart will beat and burn,
And hang my wreath on his world-honored urn.
    Nature, they say, doth dote,
    And cannot make a man
    Save on some worn-out plan,
    Repeating us by rote:
For him her Old World moulds aside she threw,
    And, choosing sweet clay from the breast
    Of the unexhausted West,
With stuff untainted shaped a hero new,
Wise, steadfast in the strength of God, and true.
    How beautiful to see
Once more a shepherd of mankind indeed,
Who loved his charge, but never loved to lead;
One whose meek flock the people joyed to be,
  Not lured by any cheat of birth,

But by his clear-grained human worth,
And brave old wisdom of sincerity!
They knew that outward grace is dust;
They could not choose but trust
In that sure-footed mind's unfaltering skill,
And supple-tempered will
That bent like perfect steel to spring again and
thrust.

His was no lonely mountain-peak of mind,
Thrusting to thin air o'er our cloudy bars,
A sea-mark now, now lost in vapors blind.
Broad prairie rather, genial, level-lined,
Fruitful and friendly for all human kind,
Yet also nigh to heaven and loved of loftiest stars.
Nothing of Europe here,
Or, then, of Europe fronting mornward still,
Ere any names of Serf and Peer
Could Nature's equal scheme deface;
Here was a type of the true elder race,
And one of Plutarch's men talked with us face to
face.

I praise him not; it were too late;
And some innative weakness there must be
In him who condescends to victory
Such as the Present gives, and cannot wait,
Safe in himself as in a fate.
So always firmly he:
He knew to bide his time,
And can his fame abide,

Still patient in his simple faith sublime,
 Till the wise years decide.
Great captains, with their guns and drums,
Disturb our judgment for the hour,
 But at last silence comes;
These all are gone, and, standing like a tower,
Our children shall behold his fame,
 The kindly-earnest, brave, foreseeing man,
Sagacious, patient, dreading praise, not blame,
 New birth of our new soil, the first American.

JAMES RUSSELL LOWELL

The Blue and the Gray

B Y the flow of the inland river,
  Whence the fleets of iron have fled,
Where the blades of the grave-grass quiver,
  Asleep on the ranks of the dead;
    Under the sod and the dew,
      Waiting the judgment day;
    Under the one, the Blue;
      Under the other, the Gray.

These in the robings of glory,
  Those in the gloom of defeat;
All with the battle-blood gory,
  In the dusk of eternity meet;
    Under the sod and the dew,
      Waiting the judgment day;
    Under the laurel, the Blue;
      Under the willow, the Gray.

From the silence of sorrowful hours,
  The desolate mourners go,
Lovingly laden with flowers,

Alike for the friend and the foe;
   Under the sod and the dew,
      Waiting the judgment day;
   Under the roses, the Blue;
      Under the lilies, the Gray.

So, with an equal splendor,
   The morning sun-rays fall,
With a touch impartially tender,
   On the blossoms blooming for all;
      Under the sod and the dew,
         Waiting the judgment day;
      Broidered with gold, the Blue;
         Mellowed with gold, the Gray.

So, when the summer calleth,
   On forest and field of grain,
With an equal murmur falleth
   The cooling drip of the rain;
      Under the sod and the dew,
         Waiting the judgment day;
      Wet with the rain, the Blue;
         Wet with the rain, the Gray.

Sadly, but not with upbraiding,
   The generous deed was done;
In the storm of the years that are fading,
   No braver battle was won;
      Under the sod and the dew,

Waiting the judgment day;
Under the blossoms, the Blue;
Under the garlands, the Gray.

No more shall the war-cry sever,
Or the winding rivers be red;
They banish our anger for ever,
When they laurel the graves of our dead.
Under the sod and the dew,
Waiting the judgment day;
Love and tears for the Blue;
Tears and love for the Gray.

FRANCIS MILES FINCH

The Ship of State

Thou, too, sail on, O Ship of State!
Sail on, O Union, strong and great!
Humanity, with all its fears,
With all the hopes of future years,
Is hanging breathless on thy fate!
We know what Master laid thy keel,
What Workmen wrought thy ribs of steel,
Who made each mast, and sail, and rope,
What anvils rang, what hammers beat,
In what a forge and what a heat
Were shaped the anchors of thy hope!
Fear not each sudden sound and shock,
'T is of the wave and not the rock;
'T is but the flapping of the sail,
And not a rent made by the gale!
In spite of rock and tempest's roar,
In spite of false lights on the shore,
Sail on, nor fear to breast the sea!
Our hearts, our hopes, are all with thee,
Our hearts, our hopes, our prayers, our tears,
Our faith triumphant o'er our fears,
Are all with thee,—are all with thee!

HENRY WADSWORTH LONGFELLOW

☆ 77 ☆